WHISPERS OF THE SOUL

poetry *Pt* today

WHISPERS OF THE SOUL

Edited by
Rebecca Mee

First published in Great Britain in 1999by Poetry Today,
an imprint of
Penhaligon Page Ltd, 12 Godric Square, Maxwell Road,
Peterborough. PE2 7JJ

A Catalogue record for this book is available from the
British Library

ISBN 1 86226 596 8

Typesetting and layout, Penhaligon Page Ltd, England
Printed and bound by Forward Press Ltd, England

Foreword

Whispers Of The Soul is a compilation of poetry, featuring some of our finest poets. The book gives an insight into the essence of modern living and deals with the reality of life today. We think we have created an anthology with a universal appeal.

There are many technical aspects to the writing of poetry and *Whispers Of The Soul* contains free verse and examples of more structured work from a wealth of talented poets.

Poetry is a coat of many colours. Today's poets write in a limitless array of styles: traditional rhyming poetry is as alive and kicking today as modern free-verse. Language ranges from easily accessible to intricate and elusive.

Poems have a lot to offer in our fast-paced 'instant' world. Reading poems gives us an opportunity to sit back and explore ourselves and the world around us.

Contents

Brighten The Home

It needs freshening up
Is what my wife said
But I could not hear
My hearing was dead.

She came back from the shop
With the tins in her hand
I could see she was serious
She had it all planned

You do the ceilings
And I'll do the walls
We'll have a smart kitchen
In no time at all.

I didn't see why it wanted
Painting at all
After all, we only
Did it last fall.

Discretion being
The best part of valour
I went to the shed
And fetched out the ladder.

Overalls donned.
I went into action
Phew! Much more of this
And I'll need some traction

Decorating Done
I sat back to view
And I must admit
It did look like new

My wife sat herself back
On her lap was our Tabby
When she looked up and said
It's made the rest look shabby

I though Oh! Dear Oh!
She's got another notion
She's the nearest thing
To perpetual motion.

I said if you want
A really good job
Why don't we now get
The service of Bob.

Now, Bob's a professional
As you will soon see
And I prefer that he did it
Much rather than me.

Len Berry

Hannah

Today I went to a teddy bear fair
There were all shapes and sizes to compare
Antique teddies who had been through many hands
Probably some where from far away lands
Fabric and pattern to make your own ted
A teeny one for a lapel instead
Searching out a bear for Hannah age six
Sitting, their glass eyes staring - what a mix
She needs a special teddy she can love
Recently her mummy went to heaven above
Lady gave me teddy brooch specially for her
Have found a grand teddy with loveable fur
Aunt and friends knitting clothes to make her smile
Will dress this teddy in a very short while
Maybe Hannah can make a friend of this bear
Support from her daddy will always be there
As Hannah grows, her secrets teddy will keep
She can cuddle him close to help her sleep

Jenny Ambrose

Wings

I watched them in their thousands
among the hedgerows and the trees
and way down there in the meadow
in the last of the summer breeze.

As their excitement rose, to fever pitch
I looked on with a heavy heart
for I wanted to, be one of them
waiting there, for the unknown start

Then all of a sudden it happened
why and how, I'll never know
for they flew to the sky together
leaving me there, far below.

And they rose up high above me
heading on to a foreign clime
oh how I yearned, for a pair of wings
and not these arms of mine.

Dear Lord, grant unto me this boon
that I might fly
and let me ride the wild wind.

Roy Turke

The Beginning Of The End

Ferocious winds,
Earthquakes and floods.
Killers and crazy people,
Dealers of drugs.

Hatred and anger,
Violence and fear.
Telltale signs,
That the end is near.

Smog and pollution,
Corruption and war.
Acid rain falling,
On concrete floor.

No more trees,
Not a trace.
No more life,
I rest my case.

Simon Houlders

Fantasy

Last night I saw a Vision
A vision too good to be true
A vision with people on a Mission
A dream I wish to come true

In the beginning, the people were happy
And they all lived in blissful harmony
The head builder was very popular
And in their eyes could not make any blunder

Soon the people became very weary
Out went the Head builder
And in came the new head builder
But the people were soon to pay dearly

Better the devil you know
Than the angel you don't know
They were weak from starving and dying
Their voices were hoarse from crying

Swiftly, they got rid of the new head builder
And they reinstated the former head builder
This is what I saw in my vision
A vision with people on a mission.

Sammy A Adeyemi

Honour

As he looks in your face,
as he looks in your eyes,
he feels the disgrace of your family's demise.

You yourself have no honour,
you care for none,
he feels the sadness of your family now gone.

As you have no honour,
I have none too,
as your family have gone we must go too.

Amy Preece (14)

Inhabitants Of Earth

O lowly mites
The galactic crumbs of deeper years
From the far depths of time.
Caught for one brief flight
In the ambient ramblings of the morrow;
Born of Terra.

Like the spume and spray cascading
Before the initial tide and deluge,
From far beyond comprehension.
The fragments of a meson.
To grow, to demise, even before it has lived;
Forgotten.

Dwell not with awe
Upon the primitive mutterings of thy matter.
For a more profound design and eternity
Manipulates the chords;
The inspiration and belief of thy world.

So cherish and preserve the precarious inheritance
Of the past and your own creation of the present.
And forge a future where we can all live
Together forever;
Whilst, yet, there is still time!

Nelson Peters

Living To-day

The world looks bright and new,
At early morning's rise.
Fair and reborn,
As dawn enlightens the skies.

The world is rushing by,
As off it goes to earn;
Hustling, bustling,
Pale faces, all forlorn.

The world is slowing down,
As the time of toil is past.
Even has come,
And peace descends at last.

The world is ablaze now,
With myriad shining lights.
Twilight postponed,
There's entertainment to-night.

Heather Olsen

Untitled

You're my second hand city of anger,
Avarice and subterfuge courses you provide,
Only offering gossamer threads of hope,
Inequalities of life grin smugly from your eyes.

Your minefields of pedestrians I cautiously traverse,
Streets like bulging arteries, willing them to burst,
My dreams lit up vermilion, blazing in polluted sky,
A humble peasant's meal, on which you'll gladly dine.

S Lawman

My Autumn Years

Here I am at sixty years
I've had my share of heartache tears
Such a long eventful life
I too have suffered pain and strife
But when I think of all the fun
The love I've shared and moments gone
Happiness that came my way
The precious times the lovely days
Watching my own children grow
To then have children of their own
The pride I feel that they are mine
I thank the Lord a thousand times
The good things I have learned from life
Being someone's dearest wife
How lucky can a person be
To feel their love surrounding me

Jeanette Gaffney

Sabian's Dawn

The rayed moon's reflections
bathed the red and white smudged roses
with a luminous blush.

A blush exposed through naked windowpanes
as an explosion of colour,
an exhibit in a gallery.

But when fingers of light fanned the sky,
I saw it as a reflection
on an old splintered mirror.

Rosaleen Clarke

To K.T

It was cold the day I went away
down soft snow clung ankle deep
about reluctant dragging feet
just as your arms about my neck
when your tears ran rivers down my cheek
you couldn't understand my leaving
my doubts my fears my reason I
couldn't bear your heartbreak tears
we once embraced a love so strong
the tattooed scars would last so long
as blood would course my veins.
Now memory only remains.

The nightmares seem they'll never go
where they do I cannot know
locked away in my private vault
filed deep somewhere under fault
guilt knows no bounds
for like a pack of baying hounds
it hunts me down and finds me out
a thousand agonies rip me apart
grip my conscience in an iron fist
so dares me not to dream my wish:
that had I been there when you needed me,
hugged you, kissed you, when you needed me,
watched you grow with grace to beauty:
I'd need not fail you, desert you, my duty.

So cold the day I went away
down soft snow clung shackle deep
about my cold reluctant feet
I couldn't bear what I had done
though my years had yet to number twenty-one
you my sweet, my baby dear
had yet to see your second year.

Andy Cooke

Stranded In Time

Is it true unearthed memory
Can damage your trite perspective?
A lifetime's wear, folded up in
Vacuous cerebral recesses,

Can strangely reveal itself and
Become acutely relative
To peripheral experience:
Crude time's neatly-cut tresses.

I sleep soft on glass, silently
Licked by a drowsy browsing herd.
My fingers tingle as I pick
Blazing fox fur on sharp spring whin.

One memory jump starts another.
Together they jolt and burden
My curious mind, consequent -
Blind where vague recall wears thin.

Where thorned thistles prickle through
Muddied socks, I await . . . time-caught . . .
And wistfully watch the myriad
Mottled white moths rise in clear light.

Their untrammelled flight is soon
Transfigured by darker thoughts
And devil-black lobster antennae
Twitch in their hot-water plight.

Again I feel those young teeth cut
Cleanly on deaf ears of corn.
Again I smell the night alight
In burning candle wax and oil.

Stranded in time, I find those dew-drenched
Mushrooms that the downy dawn adorns
And watch where those glassy eyes
Writhe for the fisherman's toil.

Stephen Shaw

Floor Reflections

Translating gleams of radiant light
Depicting rays well out of sight
For they only shine through a perspex form
Omitting a gloss which is the norm
A sunbeam has a translucent beam
Which puts shadows on reality
And an image of one's former self
Not glorious any more
Reflecting something quite different
Right across the floor.

A Jones

Satan

Satan was a bad old bloke
Trouble broke forth when he spoke.
He was a very powerful man
And had a very long lifespan.

Now old Satan wanted glory,
He told that gorgeous bird this story.
'Now now my girl listen to me.
God is keeping something from you, can't you see?
He says you can't eat from the tree in the middle
And that if you do, you'll die
But I've got brains and know it's piffle,
And that he's telling you lies.
So if you do eat from this tree,
You won't be feeling sad.
For you will know that precious quality.
Knowing good from bad.
Won't your papa be full of fun
When he realises what you've done!
So come on babes, don't be shy,
Eat from that tree, you'll not die.'

So Eve went off and committed sin,
She tempted Adam and dragged him in!
Now when the two had ate the fruit
They wore fig leaves and hid from view,
For they ate from the tree that's sacred
Which made them realise they were naked,
When God found out.
His love turned to anger
He said to the Devil,
'You've dropped a clanger!

You've told my kiddies naughty stories,
I don't know how they believed those porkies,
Because of your lies concerning that tree,
I curse you for all eternity!'

Marsha Beck

Viva

Bueno, Bueno how beautiful
for the old and the new and
the way the wind blew.

Possible one now is all and content
for time has shown us to relent
and now the sunset tonight is the longest
from Silent Night to Buenos Tardes.

For the spices for all of the Millennium
For the sweet smell of the Rhododendron
do taste the sugar plum.

Oh Bueno, Bueno how beautiful
the old road to find the way
have at last sung the child
'Now I am here to stay.'

Susan White

The Glow Worms

With the war drawing to a close and shafts,
Fill up with contaminated sand and shale.
They'd never keep it down forever, Pratts.
We now are the few that sang many a tale,
We shall bear the blue scars upon our skin.
There is no sign to show us how to adapt,
Nor to crave a crust for our loving kin,
But show our hearts are of gold and daft.
This is our Kentucky and Derby day.
Where helmets hung upon the silver brow,
In all the tiring days they sang to say,
What will the coalman dare to allow?
His redundant trade for gas and spark.
The rarity of oil and firewood to set a light,
This frozen hell, this arctic in the dark,
Where goes my sight to see the light of Blight.
Commemorate this enemy within these lands,
So green and living creatures spring into life,
Without a care to fear the child with tiny hands,
Those cries that hastened men alike to strife.
Once dead this cluster of blackened water hole,
That shines the helmet's lamp to catch a tool,
By puffer and haulage hill coal to toil,
Along the track to shafting cage this whirlpool.
Of slime and mud and drafty drains to past,
Way to lift the bulk and send it up to haul,
And lay upon the line the cart of coals depart,
From Colliers eyes and whispers of french mail.
Is it really goodbye to all of us and families so,
Lost in petticoats and old tin snappy love,
To put a sweeter heart to eat away the merry go,
Always the Jackbit to older minds in above.
In all the ages from far and near to bite,
The soldiers of steam power in wars annoy,
Then comes the final shine, the carbonate,
In all its purity where none had nowt to say.

They closed the minds for times to come in,
And dig away the modernised driving force,
No union nor clogs to sheen afoot within,
In all the towns of cities country folk to boot.

J E Richards

Crazy Ghost

The train rolled out the station, and much to my surprise.
Down along the corridor, a band I did espy.
Musicians standing there in groups, with bugles, flutes and
horns.
The big bass drum rolled back and forth, as music filled the train.

Someone standing at the back, hit a note too high.
The band they all glared at him, then suggested, the tonic sol
far.
The tuning up completed, they stood there in a row.
Huffing and puffing sweet music, as onwards the train did go.

I stood there in amusement, enjoying every tune.
When through the door a waiter came, along with his, big
bassoon.
He asked if he could join them, when he had served the lunch.
You'll have to stand there at the back, with the bugles and flutes.

The band then reassembled, and tuned up once again.
I was singing with the band, completely out of tune.
The conductor was quite disheartened, he threw his baton down.
Someone moved up from the back, and tipped him half a crown.

It's time to have or lunch now, the conductor did declare.
He bent and picked his baton up, and saw me! Standing there.
'Who are you? He said to me, your voice caused me a pain.'
I tried to explain to him, I was the driver of the train!

We all trooped in to have our lunch, and chose from the menu
grand.
'Do not inflate yourselves just yet,' said the leader of the band.
'We appear to have no driver, driving our train!'
With consternation he exclaimed! 'It's that crazy ghost again' . . .

Audrey Johnson

Christmas

Christmas time is here again,
The season of goodwill to all men,
Christmas presents under the tree,
I wonder if there's one for me.

Christmas carols, hymns and rhymes,
How I love these festive times,
Santa will be here with gifts and toys,
But only if you're good girls and boys,

Tucked up in bed wide eyed and merry,
'I wonder if Santa will drink his sherry,'
The look on their faces as they quietly doze,
What presents will we have nobody knows.

The scream in the morning, 'oh look he's been,'
The look on their faces just has to be seen,
The surprise on their faces as they gaze in awe,
At the mountain of presents stacked up on the floor.

All the well kept secrets are now in the open,
As the mound of presents the kids start to open,
What I'd give to be a child once more,
To feel that excitement of that cold Christmas morn.

G M Rivers

Casper

He walks round the place
With a smile on his face.
He's a hip, cool cat
And he knows where it's at.
He struts and he bounces
'Cos he has all the answers.
There ain't nobody moves like *Casper.*

In his fur coat of white
He moves real tight.
In and out of the crowd
'Cos he's not very loud.
He's a hip, cool cat
Who knows where it's at.
Where it's at is a cat called *Casper.*

One eye is blue, the other is green.
Wherever he goes, he has to be seen.
He's not one of the crowd
With his head held proud.
And from head to toe
He moves real slow.
He's a real smooth cat named *Casper.*

Casper's the grooviest cat in town.
He won't go where other cats are to be found.
Casper's the leader - he sets the pace.
He's the cat who's always ahead of the race.
As his tail swings low;
When he moves real slow,
You know *Casper* has seen what he's after.

Glynnis Newboult

Words On Paper

No longer plods the ploughman
And daffodils no more
Concrete, glass and tarmac
Stretch from shore to shore.

What profit in a flower
What gain a blade of grass
The country that we used to know
Is now deep in the past.

More roads, more roads, God is the car
(With traffic now you won't get far)
No thought, no care, don't look ahead
Do as you like, we'll soon be dead.

Concrete, steel and glass built tower
A symbol grand of ultimate power
Just look around, you cannot flee
From man's blind folly and poisoned sea.

When man is gone and nature stays
Waiting for a brand new day
A few seeds root and start to grow
But man is gone, he will not know.

P C Poulton

Foam And Cotton

Comfortable on Foam and Cotton
Thinking about the World
Ice cuts like a razor tonight
How many will we lose?

Selfish Minds of Covetousness
Greed, Power and Hate
Don't look to Him to Save Your Soul
You should know it's far too late

All the things that You Possess
Were manufactured from this Planet
But You already know this
You're an Education Gannet

Sleep on Foam and Cotton
My Conscience can't be Free
I know that You'll Sleep Well Tonight
You don't know Poverty

T R P Foulsham

27

Ex Post Facto

The wing tip falters
The sky twists and bends
I uniform, conform, salute and submit
My friends are not my friends
And here there is no motion
No sour in my eyes
In silence I pray I stumble away
Their blood runs down my thighs
I draw around my hand in pencil
I don't feel normal here
They look at me, study me, fill me with drugs
And the blur begins to clear
I miss her, I miss me
They think I am a danger
The sights the sounds have made me mad
She sees me as a stranger.

Greg Chappell

The Cat And The Mouse

There once was a mouse
who lived in a house,
a very big house inbred,
he tried to pinch cheese
but the cat saw his knees
and ate him all up for
lunch.

Gemma Rowlands (15)

Mars

Homeward bound but not yet in orbit, my wife suddenly said,
Did you know Mt Olympus on Mars is the highest in the Solar
                                                    System,
Fifteen miles? I leapt light minutes, climbed three Everests
And was there a little breathless on the dusty peak
Brandishing my sand axe. Well, came the voice some distance
                                                    back,
Did you know? Yes, I said wriggling through a wormhole,
Just been there.
In the receding sun, fifteen towering miles
Collapsed and sang in shafted colour of terra firma.
A black blizzard of crows flurried afield,
Exploring the pickings of the mild mid-winder.
With desultory disorder they had a lot to explore
In fifteen miles, even as the crow flies.
Night lit slow stars and crows set course for home.
Like us, they left Mars for another day.

J H Scott

Autumn Rush Hour

Crowds in the city hurrying, hurrying,
Unseeing, but seeing interior visions
Of meals to be made or meals cooking,
Empty houses or families waiting;
Crowds in queues patiently standing
Collars up, while noise surrounds them.

Traffic jams with cars and vans,
Engines humming and revving and idling,
Buses rumbling and lorries roaring,
Fire engine in the distance wailing,
Ambulance klaxon louder and louder.
Shrieking and passing and fading, fading.

Crowds in the city hurrying, hurrying,
Listen, listen in the hubbub of noises
Of cars and lorries and buses and voices
Listen, listen - a faint, faint calling
Wild geese in the sky returning, returning.

John Morrison

The Highwayman

On a dark eerie night silhouetted against the sky
Sat a highwayman all dressed in black - his name was Jack
His horse stood proud and quiet as he waited for his master's
command
He snorted nervously sharpening his hooves upon the ground
'Steady, Jess' for that was his name as he reached forward
he stroked his mane.

On the cool night air there came a faint sound
Jess heard it too and pricked up his ears
'Steady, Jess' said Jack 'so you can hear it too'
'Steady, boy not just yet we'll soon be on the move'
As the sound came ever nearer it soon became quite clear
That on the horizon a coach would soon appear.

'Time to get ready, boy,' he whispered in his ear
He pulled out his pistols, on his face there was a sneer
The coach came nearer, faster, then slowed around the bend
And the highwayman stepped out and in a voice quite clear
'Stand and Deliver!' Was the cry upon the night air
The coach came to a sudden stop and the door opened wide
And a vision of loveliness stepped from inside
He looked into his lover's eyes and too late she realised
She fired the fatal shot as in her arms Jack died.

D J Evans

Uncle's Folly

Here is a story about a carbuncle
This particular one belonged to my Uncle.
The one that he had was angry and red
Like all carbuncles it 'ad no 'ead.

The world and his wife commented on its size
But to let him hear this, was not wise.
'Cos the pain and agony makes him dance
Tho' he's too scared to go under the lance.

'Hey guv' the street urchins call
'That on yer neck, is it a golf ball?
To keep it there you must be a wag
Other golfers keep theirs in a bag.'

The offending eyesore just grew and grew
Uncle, at his wits end, pondered what to do?
Walking around town he felt a right wally
Everyone labelled the carbuncle Uncle's Folly.

That there carbuncle took over his life
Oft' coming between him and the wife.
One day she said, full of remorse
Carbuncle must go, or I sue for divorce.

Still feared to subject the folly to the knife
Tearfully, he said goodbye to the wife.
Put his affairs in order, made a will
Then got ready for that cemetery on the hill.

The day dawned when they were both past their best
Carbuncle and uncle were gently laid to rest.
Multitudes came from miles around
To see the odd shaped coffin put into the ground.

Fame, fortune and World renown
That's what the folly's brought to our town.
Postcards and photos of the great carbuncle
Has made the town prosperous, but alas, not uncle.

Ernie Jacob

Dance With A Star

Expertly dancing
With grace and such flair
We really do make
A wonderful pair
Our intricate steps
Fast flowing and smooth
Swirling and swaying
Perfecting each move
The rhythmic music
We tapped out with glee
Is all this really
Happening to me
Fulfilling my wish
To dance with a star
Whom I have worshipped
So long from afar
Hazy dream sequence
In silver and gold
As my heroes arms
Around me enfold
A grand finale
That ends with a kiss
Two figures entwined
In romantic bliss
I hear a bell ring
And I want to weep
Damn! That alarm clock
For breaking my sleep

Patricia Whittle

The Magic Of Words

The magic of words is everlasting.
Down the years, and across kind.
They resound in hearts and mind.

Despite the efforts of radio sound.
The images of film, and television.
To oust words as a vision.
Of communication beyond words.

The magic remains unimpaired.
Although tried to be lured.
To the other's lairs.

H M Etta Lewis

Untitled

Her soul doth ache
With him not near
The stagnant air
Does choke her stare,
The moon at night
Of dust does glow
Shadowed by the clouds
Now so,
Disappearing night by night,
Soon the sky will not be bright
But black and deep
And empty till
The moon returns
To calm her still.

Helen Knibbs

This Life

You are born unto this life innocent.
A life full of endless possibilities.
Never knowing which way the
Pendulum will swing.

One moment saturated by utter despair,
The next consumed by sheer happiness.

But how much of each will we get?
No one knows.

It depends on the hand that fate has
Dealt you or perhaps which way you are
Pushed.

Make the most of this life, for you get only
One.
Marvel at the beauty of this world and
Lament at man's inhumanity to man.

Learn from your experiences, for there
Can be no greater lesson.

Savour this life.
Immerse yourself within its diversity.

A Holness

A Trip To Santa

I was a little bit late
When I reached the school gate
The kids were waiting by the door
They looked up at me
Their joy clear to see
And they let out a mighty good roar

'Auntie' they cried
We were waiting inside
For our Mummy to come collect us
We didn't expect you
But of course you will do
So long as you didn't forget us

I told them our plans
As I took their hands
While listening to giggles from the two
We left the school ground
And soon we were found
In the middle of the Santa Claus queue

They gave a big grin
When at last they were in
The grotto and its colourful glory
They saw big furry bears
Snowy rabbits and some hares
Who were telling a fairy tale story

They sang us a song
As we walked along
'till we reached the end of the line
Before too long more
Elves opened the door
And we entered the Santa Claus shrine

Their eyes were glistening
As they stood listening
When Santa asked what they'd like
They smiled very brightly
Then said very quietly
They'd each like a good mountain bike

As we said goodbye
Santa said he'd drop by
With their presents on Christmas eve night
So off home we went
The letters now sent
And two children full of joy and delight

Una N Chribin

Ascension

Visited by the Holy Spirit
Lord and giver of all Life,
Christ our ever present parent,
  In mystery unique
A body you form,
  New people exist
Your spirit, unable to resist,
Newness your children enrich
  Human conditions transcend,
Channel and source of
  Multiple gifts,
Radiance and beauty of
  Creative power
In communion and mission
  A living organism,
Articulation of joints,
  Sinews, intellect,
One in equality, dignity,
  Artisanship -
Complementary, priest, lay folk,
  Religious, truly related,
  Intimately bound,
Living organisms of salvation
Serving the Divine Word,
  Visible
Everlasting sacrament for all people,
  Noble in convergence,
Saving unity, holy apostolate
Absorbed in transcendence,
  Man's sacramental nature
  Through the Spirit's presence,
      Visible,
Living, social cohesion,
Renewing, richly adapting

Human aspects in 20th century strife
  In sevenfold sacramental life,
Intimately bound in communion of mission,
  Your Spirit,
  Unable to resist.

Nora M Davidson

Secret Feelings

There's a corner of my heart
  that no one ever sees.
A corner of my heart,
  that's known to only me.

Solitude and peacefulness tranquillity abide,
  a little space throughout my life,
    where I can curl and hide.

Emotions sort their troubles there,
  true feelings tumble free.
Another world lives here within,
  and it's known to only me.

Vera Feast

A Whisper

Soft music, dim lights,
flowing wine of an Italian kind.
Clasping hands that won't let go.
Could the other people know?
Trance-like eyes that show desires.
Moments that would not stand still.
Hearts that know they never will.
Gentle kisses too and fro.
Could the other people know.
Unsaid words that say we know.
Whisper says it's time
To go.

M Rossi

Last Curtain Call

From one to eighty; take a bow; and then, amidst
The flow of time and tide - step back to recollections.
Some of pride and some that lack a touch of care
For others; when impatient youth with panache and
Flair; just left a whisper of despair and - undaunting
Travelled on their Way.
Then school; - where strict adherence to commanding
Rule was laid, knuckles rapped and battled wills. The
Teachers search for hidden skills - the prowess and
The constant work that she knew just seemed to lurk
In those stubborn teenage years - yet surfaced
Through frustrated tears;
Success Achieved.
First romance - imagined dreams. Heart was broken
World was ended, as love's unspoken word lay silent
On the ground. - But too soon emotion passes on its
Way to future classes - challenging - beckoning an
Older time of reckoning;
The stage is Set.
Too busy planning life it seems. No time to dwell on
Fickle dreams - and yet; a quiet nostalgia lingers
Faintly - for care free days (not always Saintly)
But laughter and the roguish fun - of memories and
Things begun - and left around - discarded - while
New ventures found their way
To true Proficiency
Now 'forward' signs have lost their glow; and
Disregarding them we go - uphill - like figures
In a 'Lowery' scene; up and down and in between
The falls, acting out success with calls 'for more'
The 'encore'
Now has Gone
As clouds are blown in gale force winds, the years
Speed by; - and like a 'Glossy Magazine belie; - the
Inner pages of an empty space the 'Editor' did not
replace;

It's Meaning

Interior glow of gossamer wings now fade - and
Empty cans of things once filled with expectations
Love and Life - are stilled. And shadows dance
In twilight haze and lost - evasive thoughts-then
Graze the meadows of the memory, and 'eighty years'
Regretfully;
Have passed.

Mary Beach-Smith

Humpty Dumpty

My mother looked down on me
  With a worried frown
A little hump
  Of pearly white
Most people preferred brown.
  A hand slipped underneath her
Grabbed me warm as I lay,
  It was the beginning of the end
For me that fateful day.
  They put me on a moving belt
With hundreds of my kind
  Graded me as one from five
Deep yellow streak inside.
  Into a box they packed me
Cracked running wounds all round
  When people saw the state of us
They dumped us on one side.
  It stated on our box
That we were fresh and new
  If you had been in box with us
You'd know it was not true.
  Eventually bought on the cheap
To be boiled in a pan
  Till I was hard not runny
Five minutes on watch hand.
  I then took a bashing
From a silver spoon
  Before a knife sliced off my head
To feed a human goon
  If I'd been broken, split in two
Dropped into a fry
  When turned over sunnyside
I think I would have died.

  R M Fallon

The Ghostly Angel

I was playing in the park one day, looking for some fun,
When who should I bump in to but the Reverend Jackson's son!
'Hello dear friend,' I said to him. 'You look a little pale.'
'Oh no! Oh no! I'm going to die!' I heard him scream and wail.
I held him up above the lake, and said, 'You're such a clown!'
He said, 'Don't drop me in the lake or I am sure to drown!'
I dropped him in the lake and felt quite pleased at what I'd done,
I suddenly realised I had actually drowned the vicar's son!
I ran home, crying on the way.
It has been such a horrid day!
I went to bed that night in pain,
And wondered if I'd gone insane.
As the clock struck midnight, a ghostly angel dressed in white came.
It said 'I bring back people from the dead and also cure the lame.
That was a nasty thing to do! You heard him scream and wail.
Fortunately the poor boy lived to tell his friends the tale.
Do you promise you will never do that again?' He said.

'Yes, but now can I please go back to bed?'

Emma Reading (10)

Contrast

They stand caressed.
By Time.
Those Ancient Portals.
Inviting the present
Into the past.
Where Camelot,
Is Camelot still.
The precious air, we breathe
Today.
Is polluted by gaseous fumes.
That exist not.
Nor cannot. In Camelot.
Where Knights of Valor.
And ladies, of Beauty
And Grace.
Will forever hold
Their treasured place.
That history doth decree.
Should be their lot.
In Arthur's, Enchanted,
Camelot.

J Murray

The Immaculate Injection

Lying on my back
gazing into virtual reality,
images of a German war,
leading me to a state of insanity.
Worries, what worries?
I am no longer questioning everything.
Peace of mind,
of a different kind
within my head the heaven's sing.
Walking on the cotton clouds,
the sun is shining, but due to stop.
The rain, it comes and hums a song,
of coloured crystal candy drops.
My thirst seemed quenched, by liquid gold,
my hunger never coming.
I wave my hand a rainbow comes,
my world is fucking buzzing.
I swift between the forest trees,
and as I search, a mystical age,
magicians, wizards, a crown, a king,
fulfil another stage.
I came upon a field of green,
and there I laid my head.
The small ones gathered all around,
I heard not what they said.
Worries, what worries?
I'm no longer questioning everything.
Peace of mind,
of a different kind,
within my head the heaven's sing.

John Cunningham

Recipe For Disaster

Take half a pound of butter
And half a pound of lard,
Now place in a bowl
And stir very hard.
Add one egg
And a spoonful of jam,
Add a pound of cheese
And a quarter of ham.
Stir in some treacle
And the juice from a lime,
Pour in some water,
A pint will be fine.
Now whisk thoroughly
Then add to a pan,
Boil gently
Then leave it to stand.
Now what is it you've made,
You'll never guess,
For you have made
An awful mess.

Marryn B Candler

Getting Away From It All!

Let's say goodbye to going to work for a while
and to the routine of everyday, to go away
somewhere on holiday for a few weeks, to laze in the
sun, to relax, have some fun.
Having a holiday is to get away from it all, leave
it behind, go somewhere different and unwind.
You'll never do it!
Even if you could, there still be reality to return to.
We dream of a few weeks somewhere quiet and
peaceful, don't we all!
Instead of getting away from it all, the noise and
chaos, we take it with us, and put it in a
different place, it's still all a rat race.
Holiday traffic, road works, dogs barking, just everything.
And when we get there, what do we hear, radios
blasting out next door.
What did we go away on holiday for!
To warm afternoon sun, to have peace and quiet,
and when we go to sleep at night, to hear the sounds
of waves gently caressing the shoreline.
Who are we kidding!
Perhaps the key is learning to live with it all.
What's the point of going away,
just to hear the same noise we hear at home everyday.

Linda Roberts

Six Little Mouses

Once upon a time
There were six little mouses,
And they lived in the roofs
Of other people's houses,
They all had parties,
And all ran races,
And they kept their belongings
In six suitcases.

They had very long tails,
And very long whiskers,
And three of them were brothers,
And three of them were sisters,
They wore fur coats
In the cold, cold snow,
And all of them could nibble
But none of them could sew.

So the family of mouses
Lived happily together,
Through the long summer days
And the cold winter weather,
They all gave parties,
And all ran races,
And they kept their belongings
In all sorts of places.

Now that is the tale
Of the family of mouses,
Who lived all together
In other people's houses,
They all gave parties,
And all ran races,
And they kept their belongings
In all sorts of places.

Sylvia Bryan

Untitled

Emer is my cousins name
Aiden thinks she has a special flame
They always mess around like fools
When they are together in school

They were with each other for one night only
Now both of them are feeling lonely
Emer said he had a fabulous shift
And Aiden wants to give her a gift

Someday they'll walk down the aisle
Hand in hand the two will smile
Jillian her friend is very sad
As she was into him quite bad

But don't you worry as she'll get her man
She'll do everything she can
Even call over Trevor
Which will be remembered forever

Along comes me who's into Jude
He really is quite a dude
I write him a letter everyday
But he's keeping right away

We get together in the end
About time too as he's on the mend
(It's such a long story that ends in glory
But you don't want the details in gorey)
We tied the knot at a match
Everyone says he has a good catch

Along comes Trudy who's cracked on Kevin
She thinks that he has come from heaven,
But really he has come from the bog
And he looks so much like a dog

Everyone tells her that he is gay
But she doesn't listen as they go away
Trudy wants to see the clown
But of course Kevin want to stay in Bog-town

Anon

Derbyshire

I'm not a native of this land, and have
  modestly travelled afar,

But of all the things I've done and seen
  none can match this Derbyshire,

The craggy hills and green covered tors,
  stretching back into time,

The ancient rocks before me are scarred
  with quarries and mines,

On the still clear air of morning, I hear tractors busy abroad,

Gathering hay on the lower slopes of the
  gentle long green sward,

Butterflies quickly fluttering, bright, in the heat of the sun,

Swallows on high above me, will rest when
  the long day is done,

As the sun settles like gold among the purple hills,

Leaving evening shadows cloaking those grey stone mills,

Here I know as I stand, I will never tire,

Of this green pleasant land
  they call Derbyshire.

  Sonia Jameson

Poet's Nightmare

I want to write a poem but I don't know what to say,
To ensure that it's read thoroughly and not just thrown away,
I want it to be meaningful, I want it to be strong,
Not just soon forgotten as my choice of words were wrong.

I want to express all the things in my mind.
Via paper and pen and an hour of my time,
For my thoughts to flow vividly, line after line,
Yet they don't as they're muddled, so the page stays unsigned.

The paper so white still awaits for my pen,
Still I wait for ideas as to how to begin,
Maybe a sentence, or may be a sign,
But it has to be perfect and I like mine to rhyme.

I want to make an impact and the words just must be right,
To ensure that all its readers understand inside my mind,
But as it goes it looks as if inside my head is space,
An emptiness of nothing where my thoughts just can't take place.

So I sit here, alone, still trying to write this rhyme,
Trying to express all the commotion in my mind,
Trying to clear it into words which are all mine,
Though I haven't made much impact yet, let alone a rhyme.

Aleena Matthews

Psychedelic

Mellow, relax, drift
My outside world fades
All is momentarily black
The brain, it flutters
The mind, it stutters
To those who wait, it comes.

Somewhere in there,
In those deep corridors
My celebration of light lurks
A vivid, luminous creation
The colourful curates egg
Looked by the inner sanctums doors.

Once opened, you
Will see this pit of pleasure
Languishing intensity,
But as soft as the night on the cheek
From the tails of the birds
As I experience in paradise.

Enter the pit,
Let your soul fall gracefully to it
And taste the joys of colour
No curve, no form
A spasm, an orgy
I feel no pain nor grief here.

Everything you see
Is bright and well defined
Yet not blinding or false
Just quiet, a slow
Hallucinogenic helter skelter
Without the noise of the fair

Do not forget,
Leave the doors open
The dark corridors lit
Make a ladder to the pit
As I have, follow me
Enter the door you care.

Whenever you feel
Reality let you down
Remember me and what I've taught you
Mellow, relax, drift
Let it all culminate
It's there, the psychedelic, it's there.

F Edwards

1863

In 1863
Queen Vicky did decree
her offspring Bertie find a wife
lest scandal end in civil strife

But Bert could not abide
Elizabeth of Weid
dowdy as his nurse
and not above a curse

Marie of Altenburg was handy
but she was far from dandy
Marie Hohenzollan had a pretty pout
but being catholic was out

The Weimar gells
were hardly belles
Miss Dasau tho not cold
was rather old

Dutch Marie of the Netherlands
was quite refined
but to bed confined
that left Anne of Hess
whose teeth were a frightful mess

Bertie might have gone insane
had he not found a lovely Dane
Alexandra Caroline Marie Charlotte Luise
Julie Schlesswig-Holsten Sandeburg Gluckstein

Bill Looker

You And Me

No we were never supposed to be
Together you and me,
We should have realised from the start
The pain you get from a broken heart,
It might have worked if we tried
Been good to each other and never lied.

Now that we are apart
There's a new life for us to start,
What happened in the past
All happened far too fast,
So hopefully our paths will never cross
And never again suffer such a loss.

Tony Short

The Game Of Sleep

Have you ever had that feeling,
When you cannot get to sleep,
You toss and turn and toss and turn,
For what seems to be a week.

Your pillows have gone all lumpy,
The sheets are rumpled too,
And whenever you turn over,
Your duvet sticks like glue.

You breathe in deep and heave a sigh,
Plump your pillow again,
You turn over one more time,
And decide against this game.

You sit up straight and glance at the clock,
The seconds are ticking by,
They soon turn into minutes and hours,
Which makes you wonder why?

This game you're playing is no longer fun,
In fact it's becoming a bore,
But without you knowing, tiredness takes over,
You're not playing this game anymore.

Gemma Holland

Depression

The feeling of that loneliness
Does it hide from all who see
As it takes the love of life
And other's company
Is there reasons for the feelings
That tears a troubled mind
A mind that cares for others
As the world seems so unkind
In the selfishness of self desire
What crosses do we bare
In that troubled mind of turmoil
Filled with sadness and despair
The future seems a solid wall
So high and all around
Trapped inside of all that's past
As memories abound
But there inside as hope it grasps
With your heart and all your might
Grasp on to the love of life
And fight you bleeder fight

Raymond Peter Walker

Just Once More

Toodle-pip, oh well just one more,
Then I'll stagger my way towards the door,
Goodnight sir, mind the steps as you go down,
Too late, as usual, my body hits the ground.
What a wonderful inebriated state to be in,
The vicar is dismayed at my life of sin,
So I'll just have one more, and drink to him.

Me, an alcoholic, good lord no, I can stop,
Pass me the bottle, oh dear, mislaid the top?
Never mind, shame to waste,
Better drink the last drop,
Damned good idea, don't you think, eh what!

Denyce Alexander

Epitaph

The doors swung open, the
people made a bolt, there stood
the sheriff with his '45 colt,
the outlaw stood up, and
went for his gun, he was
dead before the cloud passed the sun
O Lord protect him, and make
his path straight. Take his hand
and lead him through thy Heavenly
gates.

Barry D'arcy

The Baker's Shop

I went down to the baker's shop
To buy a loaf of bread
And just above the doorway
I saw a sign that read:-

'For sale today
As you soon will have found,
Are two scones and two doughnuts,
All for a pound'

I strolled inside the baker's shop
To see what I could find
And as I bought some doughnuts,
A man came up from behind.

'Excuse me, madam, would you like
To buy a Chelsea bun?
They really are delicious;
They turn sticky in the sun.'

I insisted that I mustn't
For I'm trying to lose weight,
But they did look so tempting
And I really couldn't wait.

I tried one that was horrible
And I decided there and then,
I knew that I would never go
To that baker's shop again!

Lisa Rawashdeh

Birthdays

The First one you don't understand why there's cards and cuddly
                                                    toys on view
Or why all the day everyone is smiling lovingly at you
By the time you're three when you awake you know this is your
                                                    special day
To open exciting parcels and make people laugh at the new
                                                    words you say

When you're five school friends come to admire your presents
                                            and share your cake
And at their parties you first realise you've got to give as well as
                                                            take
Up to ten you never stop thinking how much older everyone is
                                                    than you
But when fifteen you find you're supposed to have a much more
                                                grown-up view

Even when only twenty birthdays can cause a wistful sigh
When events happening makes you realise how swiftly time can
                                                            fly
Especially when you're a young parent with a baby of your own
                                                    to hold
Or have a young niece or nephew actually say they think you're
                                                            old

By the time you reach middle age the birthday spirit seems to
                                                            fade
Now they don't seem so important and you're happy to remain
                                                    in the shade
At eighty or ninety you begin to boast next year how old you'll be
Reach a hundred and for the first time in your life you become a
                                                    celebrity

So pass the years in which one day is a celebration of our birth
But our lives are controlled by what happens on the earth
We've got to have the strength to meet each challenge that
                                    comes our way
And still be happy to be alive when we greet our special day

J Atkinson

Nightmares

The sky grows dark,
The night is cold,
Once more we face,
Our fears of old,

You can lock your doors,
But they always get in,
So just sit right back,
And let the nightmares begin,

They're out in the darkness,
They're almost here,
There's nothing to hurt you,
But there's plenty to fear,

They come through the windows,
They come through the doors,
They come through the ceiling,
They come through the floors,

The thing in your bedroom,
The noise on the stairs,
You can pray all you want,
But they don't really care,

You can run for your parents,
You can hide in your bed,
But you'll never escape them,
'Cause they're all in your head.

Mark Cobbold

A Welcome Cuppa

There's nothing like a cuppa
  To quench a thirst,
    Of all the drinks to choose
    Tea comes first.
A cuppa tea is
  For all occasions,
    Heartbreak times
    And celebrations.
Any time of day
  Is time for a cuppa,
    Breakfast, dinner, tea,
    And even supper.
At times of trouble
  Stress and worry,
    A cuppa tea is needed
    In a hurry.
On a summer day
  When it's sticky and hot,
    What a welcome sight
    Is a brewing pot.
Tea bags, tea leaves,
  Whichever you select,
    English or foreign
    Each have the same effect.
So calming and soothing,
  Such a special taste,
    It's not surprising
    There's rarely any waste.
What a pleasure to awake
  To a nice cuppa tea
    First thing in a morning,
    Don't you agree?

Joan A Anscombe

Fantasy Lands

To the deepie we would fly
A piece of land with grass waist high
Given the name by the neighbourhood kids
We built in this land of fantasies

Playing in the land of make believe
Innocently as only children can be
Entering this paradise we would go
Our imaginations open to the flow

A house of cardboard built with flair
Apple boxes were table and chairs
Rusted tin bath became a boat
Escaping danger, climbing up ropes

Lands created in each child's prayer
Then children's eyes are not aware
They only see their mind's stories
Great adventures where dreams are achieved

The world of pretend all children try
And all to soon has to be denied
Mingled with reality as the years pass
In their mind's eye will their whole life last

Evelyn Poppy Sawyer

Princess Of The Dark

Enter the princess of the dark,
as wolfs howl and bark,
the raven he glares,
at the dark foreboding stairs,
that leads to the temple which holds the sky,
as solid as a rock but only darkness there flies,
like her cape and gown that flutter in the wind,
made from the best lace and velvet you can find.

Her pale face, her cold staring, heart chilling eyes,
send shivers down men's spines,
her blood red nails,
can cut the finest of silk veils,
lips are blue, eyes are red, a laugh like gurgling water,
leave her alone you know you ought to,
her wicked bronze golden hair,
send electric sparks into the air.

She is in every sense a vision of cold dark evil loveliness,
as she walks up the stairs to turn the key of gloom and sadness,
male domination is her game,
and to her even a tiger seems tame,
walking boldly forward up the stairs,
receiving blank, gargol like stares,
her hell bent passion can not be cooled,
not even a laughing jester could be fooled,

Up the stairs she glides,
while all the males hide,
as over her head fly the three deadly vultures,
the Lost, the Mad and the Lover,
beckoning her on with their cries,
as lightning strikes through the skies,
nothing can stop her now,
but someone please do - but how?

A lone figure races after her,
the ground behind him up in flames burns,
past her he runs and holts, and glares into those eyes of hate,
the cards unfold, it is their fate,
she stops mid stride
her heart can no longer hide,
they are now bound together, forever, below the temple in a

                                            cove,
as the key lies dormant on the floor, but don't say it will never

                                            move.

L Dyke

Giving

The world has many happy folk who smile each day
They live.
Because they've found that happiness depends on what
You give.
For a giving man is different from his neighbours in
The pod.
When his thoughts are of his brothers.
Then he's closest to his God.
And the spark of love he kindles in a breast where
Hope has died.
Sheds a warmth that's like no other.
For it feels so good inside.
And every time he gives a bit, he adds a little part
To that something deep within him.
That the poets call a heart.

William Price

Oh Well!

Alone in my cell
I thought oh well!
Here I'm to stay
for another day.

I cried a lot
for they had found a load of pot
and I was arrested, for the lot.

I never knew it was there
but they didn't care
my fingerprints were taken
a photograph too.

I am now a criminal
at the age of forty-two
it hurts to think
I had foolishly been used.

My vehicle compounded
my passport abused.

I now await the outcome
of this sordid affair
as I sit alone
in this cell so bare.

Susan Appleby

Happiness Is The Hardest Emotion To Find

Happiness is the hardest emotion to find.
Although you say I am wrong, you just wait and see.
People who say they are happy, are only so for a few moments.
Picking brief moments does not, bring you full contentment.
Your soul needs emotion all of the time.
Never a second is wasted, to get up to Heaven's emporium.
Escalators going up, reaching happiness; I do hope so.
Scaling above all other emotions, oh, being happy is so
important.
Sadness is not allowed here, it's an opposite emotion, it's so anti.
I want to give you the secret, but you have to earn it, I'm told so.
Spoiling their Heaven by those not deserving, are not allowed in.
Though for me, everybody should at least be given the right.
Happiness will be with you forever. I tell you so.
Everyday forever and ever, happiness achieved; only if.
Heaven is happiness, but you must deserve this as I.
Against the odds on this bad world, it's not difficult to begin.
Really, you should try, be happy all the time: don't be sad!

Andrew Oliver

Elvis King Of Love

You'll always be my 'Big Hunk O Love'
even though you're now with the Lord above.
I love you with my heart and soul.
'It Hurts Me' when people say you've had your day.
'What'd I Say?'
Well, if, I were 'Long Tall Sally'
or 'Lawdy Miss Clawdy'
I'd 'Wear Your Ring Around My Neck'
and if anyone should try to take it
then by heck!
I'd do a 'Rock-A-Hula-Baby'
and drive them all crazy.
Your 'Honky Tonk Angel' I'd now love to be
but I know that's the 'Impossible Dream'.
'I'm Gonna Walk Dem Golden Stairs'
so 'You'll Never Walk Alone'
and you can 'Lead Me, Guide Me'
and 'Stand By Me'
'For Ol' Time's Sake'.

Helen Barrie

Keeper Of The Kingdom

Out of darkness rays of light
shadowy fade away
the keeper of the kingdom stirs
to herald in the day
colours golden on the wing
reach out upon the morn
the keeper of the kingdom cries
light has brought the dawn.

T Neal

Imagination

I travelled to the land of no no
where fun and excitement abound
I travelled on foot through the air
though my feet never left the ground

Once there I met a friendly dog
animals all around
they came in all colours and sizes
and some could completely astound

This dogs name was Ali Kabar
his colour bright yellow and pink
he had a red patch on his back
his eyes the colour of ink

There were mice, voles and other small things
animals that live underground
there was dancing music fun and games
it gave the most wonderful sound

There was a lion preening itself
its mane the colour of blue
in the corner a snake that danced
the rumba and samba on cue

I asked if I'd been invited
or just stumbled on this wonderful time
the gold spotted pig told me
it's for people with rhythm and rhyme

For those with imagination
there are more wonderful things to see
like the singing cows the bats that hum
and the warblings of the bee

I'm going again at party time
I don't know when it will be
but I've got rhythm and I've got rhyme
so an invite they'll be for me

I'll tell you about my journey
across the land and sea
if you're feeling blue you can come too
your travel will be free.

Sheila Graham

False Alarm

I lay awake and tossed all night,
couldn't sleep, so filled with fright
was I that new life stirred within me
a whole new world of cares that would be

How was I to carry on?
My working life would soon be gone
resources low - nowhere to go
he won't want us - this I know

He said at the start
there'll be nothing for us
but my heart disagreed without any fuss
I wanted to love him and love him I did
forgive me my love - I did, I did

Dear little child, this isn't fair
you should be wanted, don't despair
I'll do my best - just count on me
and love will be yours in a-plenty.

Barbara Faye Sopp

Wander

O fishes would you welcome me,
If I fell into your deep deep sea?
And if swim my arms could do not well,
Would you me where to rest at night, so tell?
And eagles as they soar so high,
My friends be, if but I could fly?
Then if my legs be not too strong,
To carry me more miles along,
Would the grass that grows e'er 'neath my feet,
Provide me with a noon-day seat?
Would that mountain up in the sky,
Let me it climb, and with my eyes to try
To see whate'er had been unseen,
And look back at where I had been?
Through the sun and rain and clouds
        that run their race,
It isn't such a bad old place!

Alistair McLean

A Zoological Fantasia

The Iguana
The gaudily coloured iguana
Resides, so I'm told, in the Savannah.
It lives on insects
Which it carefully inspects,
But it will not disdain a ripe banana.

The Albatross
A whimsical bird is the albatross;
Feeds its young on seaweed and moss.
When they pitifully object,
Each is solemnly pecked.
'Now lads, don't make daddy cross.'

The Sparrowhawk
Another old bird is the sparrowhawk.
From the moment it's born it can walk.
But it prefers to be cute
And play arpeggios on the flute
While its brothers just sit there and gawk.

The Great Horned Toad
The stupid great horned toad!
Always walks in the middle of the road.
When told by a stranger
That its life was in danger,
Replied; 'You don't say. I'll be blowed'.

The Flamingo
The aristocratic flamingo
Will have nothing to do with the dingo.
He plays, so they say,
A superb game of croquet
And is a wizard at winning at bingo.

The Porcupine
The prickly natured porcupine
Delights to take a glass of wine.
But if a drop of it you spill,
It will stab you with a pointed quill
Muttering gruffly 'Rotten swine'.

The Giraffe
You must never, never laugh
At the long necked giraffe.
Or from his great height
He will kick with all his might
Wearing the supercilious smile of a seraph.

The Cassowary
Be very, very chary
Of approaching a cassowary.
If he doesn't like your face
He will spit and then give chase
And kick you all the way to Londonderry.

The Golden Carp
The beautiful golden carp
Is a connoisseur of the harp.
But it's certainly very queer
From the stories that we hear
It can't tell a flat from a sharp.

   K C Cleak

Untitled

How strange the unplanned
sudden meeting that comes
with sweet surprise it lights
ones heart with such happiness
which is difficult to describe
unless you see a rainbow,
reaching across the sky.

Elizabeth D Perrin

Lost City - Atlantis

Sunset dawn in paradise, a rhapsody of joy,
Marvelled at, magnificence, on Heaven's gates, did stand.
This wondrous, lost, utopia, this long forgotten land,
Idyllic city, heart of dreams, a glittering metropolis,
In sparkling splendour, gilt-edged moon, your elegance beguiles.
Oh! Beauteous, long, lost, paradise, beneath the raging seas,
Thy pride, thy greed, and decadence, did bring Thee, to thy knees
And lost forever, sunset dawn, or but a waking dream?
Long down the mists of time they call, they whisper on the
                                                    breeze,
Those lost, forgotten voices, ring they shall not take their ease,
Forever held in time, to speak, of lost elusive land,
That marvelled at, magnificence, that on Heaven's gates, did
                                                    stand!

Angela McLaughlin

The Mary Rose

At a grand council chaired by 'enery the eighth,
'A great warship I want bilt' he sayth,
'With cannon and ball and masts quite tall,
A solid plank and that's not all,
The finest equipement for the keel-haul.'
The Mary Rose.

The plans then drawn to the king were shown,
His majesty examined them from the throne.
Came a cry of delight, then shouted with ease
'Gadzooks and odds bodikins, they do me please!'
The Mary Rose.

Each man worked hard his work not shoddy,
To ensure his head remained attached to his body.
From dawn to dusk they toiled away,
To be finished by a specific day.
The Mary Rose.

When all was done the ship moved out,
Manoeuvred by the captain's shout.
Direction came forth by the score
To impress his majesty on the shore.
All the crew rushed up above,
To wave farewell to those they love.
And with banners flying and mothers crying.
The Mary sank.

Robert Barnes

How Much More Tar, For Your Car?

Metallic and metal
And made from the earth
I wonder how much
Your vehicle's worth
We buy them from people
Who give us the spiel
They give you the contract
To wrap up the deal

You wash it and wax it
And polish it with cloth
The next time you drive it
There's suicide moths

We drive on this black stuff
Just laid for your car
The countryside's criss crossed
With bitumen tar.

And then on the day
That the banks are all closed
We drive to the seaside
And snarl up the roads

We drive on these roads
And head for the town
We have to go through
Cause there's no way around.

We fill them with petrol
And drive everywhere
We race round the roads
And pollute up the air.

We drive them like roadhogs
They fill us with rage
We use them as weapons
And sometimes get caged

So next time you driving
Your automobile
Just think how those poor
Pedestrians feel

P M Ritzkowski

Horses For Courses

Whatever type of employment you're in
You can pick it out with a pin
Always with some sort of force
That you must attend, the course
Seats all around in a tight room
People sitting full of gloom
Not knowing what is likely to transpire
But there is always, the one live wire
If management you need to act
This is a known and amazing fact
Role playing is the order of the day
Although it often brings dismay
Being aggressive is no real deal
But it depends on just how you feel
The tutor needs this type of behaviour
Even if you are not in favour
This is to bring one to your peak
As courses tend to last the whole week
Having managed that awkward bit
It's now time for you to have a sit
Back and watch the others be a fool
One wonders whether this be a useful tool
When working in one's office space
Back at the work place
There are so many extra forces
When gathering all the horses for courses

Anthony Higgins

Get On Quickly

Can you get on more quickly
You seem kind of slow
I need this job doing
Before other places I can go.

Can you get on more quickly
You seem to talk all day
And seem to have so many things
Apon the floor in your way.

Can you get on more quickly
For the job looks so small
Enough to have finished
Before home time comes to call.

Keith L Powell

Anchors Aweigh

As the command is called to the seamen to
Weigh anchor in all of the great ships of the sea
When all of the chain brings the giant anchor
To its recess so very sturdily
The chain composed of links that must hold the
Vessel fast where it is at rest
Or when violent storms cause great waves to
Rock these giant ships with their crest
These chains will take the total strain against any
Strong adversary winds
Being forged the links are fused by blacksmiths whom
Bend the red hot metal to ensure each solid end
In bygone days the links were a solid bar then
Heated white - then beaten into shape to fit into the link bend
Handling the hot metal caused these devoted
Smithies with their helpers to perspire
Oatmeal was immersed into a bucket of water for them
To quench their thirst to combat the heat of the furnace fire
Such ardent people whom completed this tedious task
So thorough so true
Such patient labour to ensure our ships to sail
The seven seas blue
Ever sure of every link that they forged will
Last eternally
To hold our ships steadfast where ever they may-be

Douglas Fudge

Jill Of All Trades

I'm Jill of all trades
and mistress of none
but in all of my jobs I had
so much fun

As a trainee window dresser
to work I went
my wages, seventeen shillings
I had already spent

Next to a chemist to sell
pills and potions,
lovely perfumes, lipsticks,
powders and lotions

Then as a fishmonger I had a
go,
from perfume to fish was
a bit of a blow.

Landlady, projectionist, then
a telephonist,
and a lovely four years as
a vet's receptionist

Nursing and caring I spent
my last years
living life's mixture of
laughter and tears

I'm still just a Jill and
a mistress of none,
but I hope every job
that I did was well done.

Pim Foster

The Factory Calls (a reluctant factory worker in the 1930's)

I hear the sound of footsteps in my sleep,
I dream of mountains, I see the lost sheep,
This great old city waking from its bed,
As shunting trains go shunting thro' my head.

The morning light creeps thro' the windowpane,
The birds have sung their early dawn refrain,
And early workers tread their daily way,
To the cries of young children out at play.

The factory calls, their hooter screeching high!
How white-faced workers from their houses fly.
The gate, the factory gate is open wide,
Soon to close, there are hundreds locked inside.

I see the moorlands and the mountains high,
The meadows green, the sun up in the sky.
Let them wait, let the factory bosses wait,
So let them close their ugly factory gate.

But now I find my dreams fly from my head,
No more time to dream, no more time for bed.
The gate! The factory gate is open wide!
So it seems I'll always be the last inside.

So come one day I'll break this daily tread,
I'll pack my bags and follow the sun instead.
I'll climb the mountains where they touch the sky,
And in my dreams beneath the stars, I will lie.

Joe Kay

Sweet Sixteen

Oh, to be sixteen
And start my life again
Not to marry young
But have some fun instead
For if I had listened to my parents
When they told us to wait
Not brushing off what they said
Now it's far too late
For once the children
Start to come along
He blames all this on you
You can't return to mum
And should he hit you
You wonder what you have done wrong
But you can't walk away
And leave your children behind
Then bad names he calls you
Which you can't print this time
He looks to other women for his fun
Sometimes buying their time
And he hurts you even more
Did you really care?
Then one day happiness
Knocked upon your door
Did you stop loving your children?
Oh, no not you
But they caused you unhappiness
And also lots of pain
For they had listened to dad's new woman
And her lies, over and over again
But deep within my heart
I've never stopped loving them
And I hope this kind of hurt
Never comes their way
For I gave them life

And am here if they need me
Till Jesus calls me
And peace comes my way
Forever and a day!

Pauline Haggett

Memories

A leafy glade, spring water rushing
Cool droplets spray the dusty earth
Tiny bird waiting, my footsteps hurried
Sends it flying to the wood
Cobbled stones make hard the footpath
Passing by the trees and shrubs
Bringing back my childhood memories
Of fun and laughter in this wood

Passing down the pathway onward
Tall dark pines on either side
Mossy stones and deep brown cones
A stile to climb, I feel alive
Wandering through the fields a yonder
Coming now to waterfall
Old, neglected, stones and rubble
Fill what once was clear and cool

Moving on along the pathway
Upward steps of wood and stone
Leading to the lake of memories
Yellow lilies, reeds, primrose
Oh, the peace and feelings
Fill me with the breath of spring
It's forty years since I last walked here
Nothing has changed this beauteous scene.

Brenda Whitby

The Hooker

it's cold on the street, the sky's dark and grey
The punters are out, and they're willing to pay
She's only fifteen, but looks thirty-five
She often wonders what keeps her alive
A punter pulls up - 'What's the damage, Pet?'
She stops and ponders, she wants all she can get
She gets in the car, and studies his smile
She hates him with vengeance, his presence is vile
Three years on the game and going nowhere
She looks back at the corner - she somehow belongs there
She can't stand his smell, the leer on his face
She wants it all over, to get out of this place
She's done three already, a busy little girl
Life is a buzz - one long social whirl
He grunts and he fumbles, there's a tear in her eye
Five minutes of pleasure, for him, no goodbye.
Twenty quid richer and back on the pull
She'll not stop working until her purse is full
She watches the pimps, the tarts and the johns
With a look of acceptance, afterall, she belongs
'One-day, one day' she says to her self
Doesn't want to get old, or left on the shelf,
She struts up and down, parading her wares
Avoiding the others, ignoring the stares.
She's hardened to this, and ready to fight
This is her pitch and she's earned the right
She'd love to get out, pack in, and retire
But she knows what she's got, and what they require
'One day, one day' - she says it again
She pulls up her collar, it's starting to rain
For now, she accepts her sordid surrounds
In the hope that one day happiness abounds.

Eddie Hunter

Cast out Your Devils

The Devil:
Who is he?
And where does he dwell?
Well, that's right down in hell
Where Paradise was lost.

The Devil:
What's he like?
A fiend or a demon,
Or all hell let loose?
Whatever he is,
And where're he abides,
The Devil is evil
All mortals should scorn.

Yes, devils abound,
Where're we may be,
They tempt us,
Molest us,
And ruin our lives,
So make no room in your hearts,
For these devils at all.

Cast out all your devils,
Cast out everyone.
Those devils of hate, anger, malice and lust,
Plus spite, greed and envy,
Vanity and pride:
For these are the devils,
That wreck all our lives.

This earth would be Eden,
With no devils at all:
No devils to ensnare us
To encompass or possess us;
Leave no room, I implore you,
Cast them out, one by one,
And I'm sure by so doing
We'll regain Paradise.

Victor S Barrett

Mermaid

I dreamed I was a mermaid
Swimming under the surf.
The sky was azure
Through the waves.
And I was free,
And beautiful,
And safe from the outside world.
It was a wonderful feeling
I can't describe it
I want to hold it forever in my heart
And share it with you -

Jane Findlay

Memories

Sweet dreams are made of
memories that flutter through
your mind.
They stare you in the face.
But you cannot see when
you are blind.

The flowers that dance in
the morning dew that seem
to call out to you, and
starts you with another dark day -
and what you would give to see
the sun and have a little fun.

To be able to play for just
one day would be a dream
in itself come true.

Sharon Singleton

Memories

My Mother is no longer here
memories of her I hold so dear
her kindness and love to everyone she gave
her smile and gentleness she took to the grave

She was always there to comfort and guide
always there by my side
a rare and wonderful being with so much love and giving
blue skies or rain I still feel the pain
I miss her so very much I miss her gentle touch
her photo by my side my tears I cannot hide
I whisper her name, will life ever be the same

I like to think she's in a better place
an angel full of love and grace
or a star shining so bright
her presence I feel day and night
it's many years since mum has gone
but for her I still long

Rock of ages she did love
now she's singing in heaven above
God's love she deserves
for her goodness over the years
one day we will meet again
our joy and love shall reign

Barbara Geatches

Time

Remember the happy old school-days, and the old ticking clock
on the wall,
the lessons would go on for hours - except when we all played
football.
The teachers would sit at their high desk and hammer in dull
history,
as we could all count off the seconds - our only ambition was
tea.

When school-time was over we'd run out to play all lessons but
maths we'd forget
which seemed to pop up several times to calculate odds on a
bet.
The days would drag on as we watched the old clock why didn't
they take it away,
but as we grew older with more things to do we needed a thirty
hour day.

The years all sped by taking months and the weeks, we have
time now to sit, and take shock,
the children grow up, and their children, did They watch that old
ticking clock.
The older we get so the time flies, it really does not seem quite
fair -
we have time now to do what we want to - but somehow the want
to's not there.

Don't watch the old clock and its ticking just stretch the whole
day to its full,
enjoy springtime and summer and winter - looking back, there's
not one day that's dull.
Father Time controls that old ticking clock Not the problems that
We generate,
but we have a chance to keep him in check, so enjoy life - and
tell him to wait.

Jim Pritchard

Memories

When I travel in my mind to yesterday,
And relive the days of yore.
I meet once again all the folks that I loved,
Who sadly are no more.
True happiness dwells within my thoughts,
I laugh with the family, now gone.
Remembering times before I was sad,
Times when the sun still shone.
We were once a large happy family,
There is nobody left now but me,
But one day when I find my heaven,
What a glorious reunion there'll be.

June Ball

Living Memories

What a marvellous thing, the mind can be,
The pictures it paints for you to see,
Just close your eyes, and you will find,
The things you thought you had left behind.

Friends may die, and pass away.
But in your mind, they will always stay.
Many things in life have come and gone.
But memories, will always live on.

The things you loved, to touch, and hold,
A life more precious than any gold.
The things you think, may make you cry,
But memories will never die.

You may be young, you may be old.
Just remember the stories you've been told.
A laugh, a smile, and many a tear.
These memories you need never fear.

Memories may be all you have got,
Some are good, a few are not.
But cherish them with love, and care,
They could be all you have to share.

The things you did, and those you knew
Are always very close to you.
The life you live, I hope will be
A long, and happy memory.

Kenny Boy

A Christmas Truce

They said by Christmas it would be all over
War be won and back home to Blighty,
But we sit here in trenches miles from Dover,
Praying each night to God almighty.

We wait another day in vain for orders
Winter rains drop a foot of water,
Is it really we who dispute the borders
Ladders poised to ascend to slaughter?

Each day guns thunder, shells fly past on heading,
Men like us target for mass killing,
Fired in return German cannons are shedding
Death on those who took the King's shilling.

It's eve of Christmas and those shells stop winging,
Silence reigns as though by God's accord,
From German trenches sound of voices singing
Christmas carols praise the birth of the Lord.

Heads then bodies rise with guns held handy,
Cautious calls for us to share their drink,
Exchange God's greetings as we sip a brandy
Comrades in a nightmare none can shrink.

A brief rapport to play a game of football,
No animosity, made brief friend,
Time passed too swiftly, soon shouts heard for recall,
A pity that *this* day had to end.

With Christmas over now it's back to fighting
Officers order the next advance,
Men illuminated by shell blast lighting
Final sacrifice, war circumstance.

Behind the lines lie heroes, wound bound dressings,
No more war for them they've won release,
Each will remember friends and thank God's blessings
When next *they* celebrate Christmas peace.

William Smith